Fantasy Workshop

A PRACTICAL GUIDE

BORIS VALLEJO AND JULIE BELL

Fantasy Workshop

A PRACTICAL GUIDE

TEXT BY NIGEL SUCKLING

First published in Great Britain in 2003 by Paper Tiger

The Chrysalis Building
Bramley Road
London W10 6SP

An imprint of **Chrysalis** Books Group plc

1 2 3 4 5 6 7 8 9

ISBN: 1-84340-118-5

British Library Cataloguing-in-Publication Data: A catalogue
record for this book is available from the British Library

Designed by Paul Wood

Colour reproduction by Classic Scan, Singapore
Printed by Imago, Singapore

CONTENTS

Wolf's Eyes

Julie has a particular fondness for wolves, as can be seen elsewhere in this book and other collections of her work. Working to publishers' commissions often allows artists to pursue their own interests at the same time.

Introduction

All the books I have done with Boris and Julie have been adventures of one kind or another, but this was the best one yet because we finally got to meet for the first time. It's surprising really that we managed so well before by just chatting on the transatlantic phone. But this time it simply wasn't working, so the publishers flew me across to Philadelphia to stay with them for a week.

The first thing to say is that Boris and Julie's dedication to art is only matched by their charm and hospitality. I had a wonderful time and the book just naturally took shape as you see it. I had the chance to watch over their shoulders as paintings materialized and any budding painter will find a wealth of insights given here into how they go about their profession. You don't have to be an aspiring artist though to appreciate what they have to say and show. If you just happen to like their paintings you should find your understanding of them deepened enormously by seeing the meticulous thought and care that goes into their creation. This is described mostly in their own words because they are very articulate about what is, after all, a mostly non-verbal practice.

Some years ago Boris published another book on fantasy art techniques that is still very popular and the aim of this one is not to replace it but to pick up where the other left off. There is inevitably some crossover but you do not need to be familiar with that one to enjoy this. Conversely, if you know the other book you shouldn't suffer too much déjà vu with this. They simply complement each other.

Preparation

1. Priming the board
2. Taping the board to stiff backing
3. Masking the painting area
4. Pressing down the edges to prevent seepage

CHAPTER ONE

Preparation

PREPARING THE BOARD

The first step with any painting is having a good surface on which to work. Because their pictures are not usually very large – 20 × 30 in (50 × 76 cm) is typical – Boris and Julie do not use canvas for their illustrations as the texture of even the finest canvas interferes with fine detail. Some painters use wood or Masonite to overcome this but these are heavy and therefore difficult to store. By choice, Boris and Julie use Strathmore cold press, double weight illustration board. This is made of 100% cotton, is acid-free and permanent. They reserve canvas for private works and experiments.

1   One problem they find with illustration board is that it is naturally too absorbent, sucking the paint in and causing it to dry too quickly. To remedy this they first prime it with three coats of Gesso, each brushed on at right angles to the previous one to avoid creating texture and left to dry before recoating. Gesso is a white acrylic undercoat that gives a nice matt surface. The large 3-in (7.5-cm) brush is dipped in water each time before being recharged to thin the acrylic a little. Having to leave each coat to dry takes a few hours so Boris and Julie generally take half a day for the job to prepare several boards at a time.

2   To resist any tendency to bowing, the Gessoed board is then taped to ⅜-in (1-cm) foam core backing, which has two layers of paper sandwiching one of Styrofoam. The boards are taped together at the edges with artist's tape (a finer and wider version of masking tape).

3   2-in (5-cm) wide masking tape is laid over this as a frame around the area to be painted.

4   Finally, a burnishing tool is used to press down the inner edge of the masking tape to prevent paint seeping under it. When a painting is complete, the masking tape is removed to give a nice clean edge, but it's important to leave the artist's tape binding the boards together so the picture doesn't curl as the paint dries.

Julie: A lot of people think that the last two steps are not important, but they give the work a professional finish.

Boris: It's less important than it used to be because now we often send our clients a digital image of the painting, but presentation still makes a difference if someone comes to buy a painting. Also it shows pride in what you do.

BRUSHES

Having prepared a surface on which to paint, the next step is to make sure you have the right brushes handy for any circumstance that might arise, because you don't want to have to rush out and buy a new brush at any critical stage of a painting. Below you see Boris and Julie's pot, although obviously their collection has built up over years of constant work and experimentation. To start with it should be enough to sit down with two small, two medium and two large brushes. One of these is for laying down areas of colour and one for blending paints on the board, going over them with a clean, dry brush to smooth the gradations of colour. In Boris's opinion: 'Blending is 50% of the painting process. Smoothness is arrived at by using a dry brush. Some areas are blended and some made really rough to get contrasts. As you get more and more experienced you learn how to decide on the balance each picture needs.'

For fine details Boris and Julie choose Winsor & Newton sable Series 7 No. 0 or 1. These are expensive, costing about $15 in the US, and they normally get through one or two per painting but it's worth it to work in the fine detail. With all brushes you save a lot of money by remembering to clean them when finished for the day.

For the larger brushes experience is the best guide to what you will need, but as a general rule sable ones are best for details and smooth blending because they don't pull paint off the board. Synthetic ones are good when this is required, for example when painting rocks and other strongly textured surfaces. In these cases the paint is left to dry for ten or fifteen minutes before the brush is dipped in thinners and wiped on a cloth, so it is just damp before being applied to the paint. The most important general rule is that you need brushes that won't fall apart in the middle of a painting so that you have to pick out the bristles, and these brushes are worth the expense.

IDEAS

The next thing you need before starting a painting is an idea of what you want to paint. Well, anyone who wants to be an artist usually has a few ideas to start with, but realizing them on canvas or board often proves harder than they imagined. It's not just a matter of technique. Here are a few tips:

Sky

1. Underpainting the composition in acrylics
2. Fleshing out the background

Boris: Two things are important to make clear from the beginning: Firstly, the more you paint, the more your brain will get used to coming up with ideas. Secondly, I don't go looking for ideas, I let them come to me. If they elude me, what I do is open my mind and wait. It's like meditation, you cannot force it. It may seem funny but often the best way to come up with ideas is not to try. Instead of racking your brains, just lie on the floor and let your mind go blank.

Julie: Trying too hard can just inhibit your imagination.

Boris: Another device is to close your eyes and imagine a TV screen with something happening on it, something related to whatever it is you're trying to capture. Just imagine you can move around in any kind of direction. The tricky thing is then to grab just one frame because you're looking for a flat picture, not a movie. When that frame comes, grab

Sky

3. Refining the background

4. Concentrating on the main figure

5. Concentrating on foreground details

Opposite: Finished Image. This picture was one of a personal series Boris and Julie undertook simply to celebrate their love of nature. At the end of each one they dropped in a title and border in Photoshop, but the main picture was simple painting in their usual manner. colour-wise, Julie consciously echoed the yin-yang symbol in which each half contains a spot of its opposite. So, the dark vegetation contains a bright flower and the bright sky contains a dark bird. The bird also gives the viewer something to identify with because, without an animal or human figure, landscapes can seem too empty.

it and you're ready to start work. The next thing is the technical aspect of putting your idea down with pencil on paper.

Julie: Another way to get ideas, if you have a specific subject in mind, is to look at anything related to it that will give you the local colour. For example, if it is bodybuilding you can flick through magazines. If it is a book cover about, say, pirates you can watch movies, look through history books, anything that will give you a general feel. You're not looking for anything specific to copy, just letting the information soak in till some idea comes to mind that you can use. You have to remember that pictures never turn out as you originally think anyway. You don't have to be afraid of copying (unless that's what you're deliberately trying to do) because wherever you start, the picture will move away from that.

Boris: That's right, pictures have a life of their own and you have to let them develop in their own way. So anything with striking images can feed your imagination – fashion magazines, art books, photographic books. When you flip through them you're not concentrating, just absorbing general impressions. It also helps to know your subject. If you don't understand what you're doing it's going to show through – you can't fake it just with technique.

Julie: For example when we were commissioned for the X-Men trading cards it helped that I had a lot of experience with comic books from years before because there are lots of subtle details to comic characters that are important to the fans. They can tell if you're faking. With a free painting it's easier. Sometimes an idea comes just from someone saying what they'd like to see in a picture. Often one just comes when you're not expecting it. You just see something that makes you think: 'Wow! That could be translated into 2D'. And you take it from there. Sometimes I see a photo and the colour and lighting might suggest a picture that has nothing to do with the subject of the photo. It might be a bowl of fruit, but to me it suggests a sorceress.

When I first started painting I once needed a background and Boris said, 'look through this book'. I did, but there but there was nothing exactly right. He said, 'that's the point, you're looking for a feeling not an exact background'. And at the end all the bits and pieces came together to make what I needed.

Boris: The point is that you're not always going to find the exact reference for what you want so you have to understand what you see rather than copy. Also, in fantasy, nature is just your point of departure because everything is larger than life. But as a general rule, the better your reference, the better your painting.

Julie: So ideas are all over the place, there's just not enough time to do them all. If ever I feel like I'm hitting a dry spot I think it's probably because I'm too uptight. I must have gotten away from myself.

REFERENCE MATERIAL

Although the starting point for Boris and Julie's pictures is usually a rough, or even quite detailed sketch, the realism of their paintings comes from a skilled use of reference material. For this they have accumulated a vast library of art and nature books, magazines – anything really that shows textures and details they may want to paint. They also photograph much of it themselves, especially the main characters of their paintings.

The camera they mostly use these days is a professional quality digital camera, a Nikon D1X, which gives as good quality images as any previous camera using film. One advantage of this particular camera is that they can change lenses. They normally use a 28-300 zoom lens that allows them to close in on a subject's face, for example, without the distortion that comes from going up close with a normal lens.

Julie: Professional equipment is great, but not a necessity. We know illustrators who use cheaper cameras; and when Boris first started he just used a cheap Polaroid and still managed to produce beautiful paintings.

Above: To understand how to paint shiny metal, collect photos of simple examples rather than trying to paint directly from the objects. Photos allow them to be seen as patterns of colour that can then be simplified.

Right: Any interesting reference shot might later find its home in a painting.

One beauty of fantasy is being able to play with scale so, as here, a lump of crystals that you can easily hold in one hand can become a mountain in the distance. At the same time purely natural wonders like the sunset sky, opposite, can be celebrated in fantasy simply by introducing a fantastic element like a fairytale castle or perhaps a unicorn.

Boris: Being professionals we've built up our equipment little by little, but most consumer digital cameras now give really good-quality pictures. Maybe we could say here that although we always work with models and reference material for finished paintings, we don't just copy the photos as they come out. Figures will be made longer or more muscled or whatever to suit the aim of the painting.

Here is the studio in the basement of their home where Boris and Julie usually photograph their models.

The large roll of paper hanging down in the basement studio is used to produce a neutral background in front of which they photograph the subjects of their paintings. Frequently two light banks are aimed to light the figure from both front and back to produce shadows that bring out the three-dimensionality of the subject. Harsher lighting is less flattering than soft lighting but gives more detail, which helps you to produce a better painting. Usually more information is needed when the photo is going to be the basis of a painting.

The light banks Boris and Julie use are stroboscopic, giving a brief burst of intense light for each shot. Floodlights could be used instead but have a more limited range of control; they are necessary however if you don't have a professional camera designed for use with strobes.

On this blank stage models are posed with any props that can bring them closer to whatever they are trying to represent. Opposite is a selection of battle props ranging from genuine antique weapons and authentic replicas through to fantasy swords, some of which were designed by Boris and Julie themselves for the Franklin Mint. This prop basket is always a magnet for visitors and a great aid to getting models in the right mood.

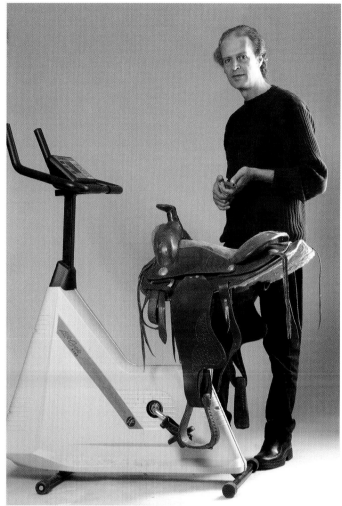

Props lend realism to a pose and an exercise bike can stand in for a horse.

On occasion Boris and Julie will hire a model and shoot off a lot of pictures without any purpose in mind, hoping that later they will either suggest a picture or fit in with something they need. More usually though they have a particular pose and attitude and character in mind and get a model to act the part, along with as many suitable props as they can find, not only because it lends realism to the pose, but because it saves looking for reference material from elsewhere later. One useful prop that has often stood in for a horse is an exercise bike and here you can see your author making like Jesse James with a Colt 45 and saddle.

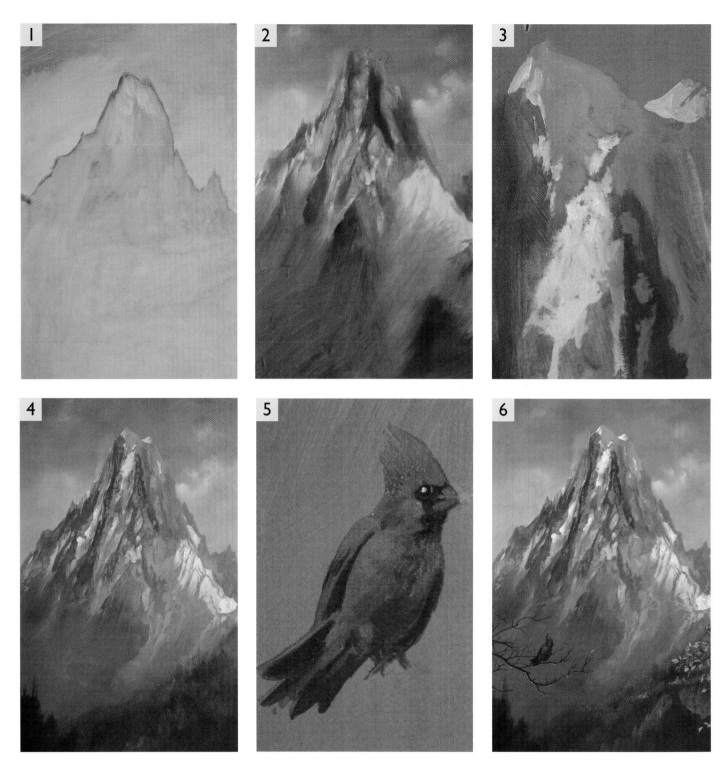

Mountain

1–6. Details of Mountain, shown opposite page

Opposite: Finished image. Boris – When I paint rock I don't like to render it in any detail, I prefer to give my brush a free hand and just let things happen. In this particular painting the colours are mostly very cool and needed some warmth by way of contrast, so I introduced the red bird.

Story Teller

1. A little dragon is added after the main figure has been sketched out

2 & 3 inset. Details are strengthened in sienna acrylic

CHAPTER TWO
Realizing Ideas

TRANSFERRING IMAGES TO BOARD

Once Boris and Julie have a suitable shot of a model for a painting, they print it out in sepia tones at the size they intend to use it, then make a line drawing on tracing paper from the photo, which is kept handy for being referred to later on. The line drawing is then placed face down on a light box and another piece of tracing paper is laid and a copy is made. This gives a reversed image from which they trace what is needed for the painting with an HB pencil. This tracing is taped face down onto the Gessoed board and rubbed over with an 8H pencil that transfers it to the board facing the right way. Here are two examples:

1 In this case Julie initially transferred the main figure to board without having a clear idea of what the creature on her wrist was going to look like. So she went back to the original drawing, worked out what it looked like on the tracing paper and followed the same procedure to transfer it to board. As this was for a calendar picture, she had a very free hand and so only began on the background after the lady and her pet were sketched out. Usually with commissioned pictures the client will have had to approve a detailed drawing of the whole picture before painting goes ahead.

2 3 The initial sketch was then fleshed out with shadows in burned sienna acrylic paint, which seals the pencil to the board, unlike oils which smear it.

Story Teller

Finished image

Boris: It's important to note that this image was for a calendar so it was a very loose concept that could be developed as it went along. This is a very different way of working than with a commission that is all decided beforehand.

1 In the case below Julie wasn't sure of the costume, so she started without any so she could improvise with the picture in place. Again, this was for a calendar so she had the freedom to experiment as she went along.

2 You should just be able to see the tracing paper taped to the board for working out the costume. The reason for not working directly on the board is that erasing lines leaves a residue on the surface that will affect the painting later; so it removes a worry, even though it usually means extra work.

Boris: Tracing paper is very important in our work because you can experiment as much as you like without harming the end painting. We work out all the problems on tracing paper before putting the image on the board.

3 **4** The same process is gone through with the background, although with buildings like these (pages 26–27) it's often enough just to trace in the basic shape and improvise the details in paint on the board. The wolves were photographed at a sanctuary not far from where Boris and Julie live.

1

2

Enchanted Pack

1. First sketch without a costume

2. Tracing paper overlaid on board for sketching

3

3. Costume details worked out on paper

4

4. Costume transferred to the board

OVERALL PLANNING

When creating the elements of a picture, Boris and Julie start by considering the main form – be it a mountain, tree, creature, rock or whatever. Each of these has an intrinsic nature, but because this is fantasy they also like to combine these elements, for example to inject organic elements into a rock formation.

When planning a picture the first consideration is the overall shape, which is fleshed out with solid shadows to make it three-dimensional. Then you go into sub-forms and surface textures, as can be seen in the rock detail opposite.

Boris: For example, with a tree trunk there will be certain areas of sharpness that can be shown in the edge-line. You don't want the same colour throughout because that's not what you see in nature. Also, you should exaggerate details to make the form stronger. In rock, for example, you will have different minerals side by side, so this should show in painted rock. One method we use is to let the base colour we have applied dry for a while and then dip the brush in turpentine, wipe it on a cloth so it is just damp, and then use to lift off patches of colour. It's a very spontaneous process – you have to let the shape of the rock emerge on its own. Then you go in with a small brush to accentuate the details.

1. Painting in the background
2. Detail of insect form

Lost City

Lost City is a good example of where the rock looks organic and muscular but is also obviously solid stone. Also, besides the giant wasp, insects inspired the structure of the buildings in the background of the main picture. One of Boris's hobbies is photographing insects and, one way or another, they often find their way into his pictures because, he says, they are an alien life form living right under our noses.

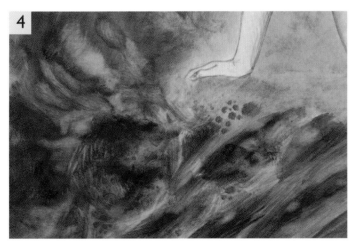

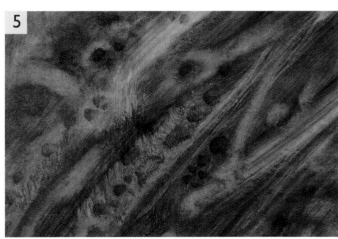

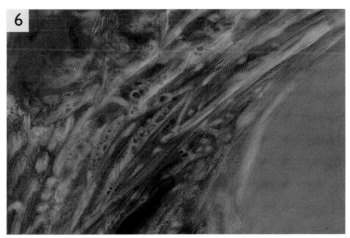

3. Insect forms injected into the buildings
4, 5 & 6. Organic forms blended into the rocks

7

7. The human figures are painted in last. When they are finished, attention is given to completing the background.

Opposite: Finished Image. The photo realism of the main figures in Boris and Julie's pictures is what makes the overall scenes so plausible, but the portraits are not always as lifelike as they seem. The photos they start from are often exaggerated or modified to suit the situation and setting.

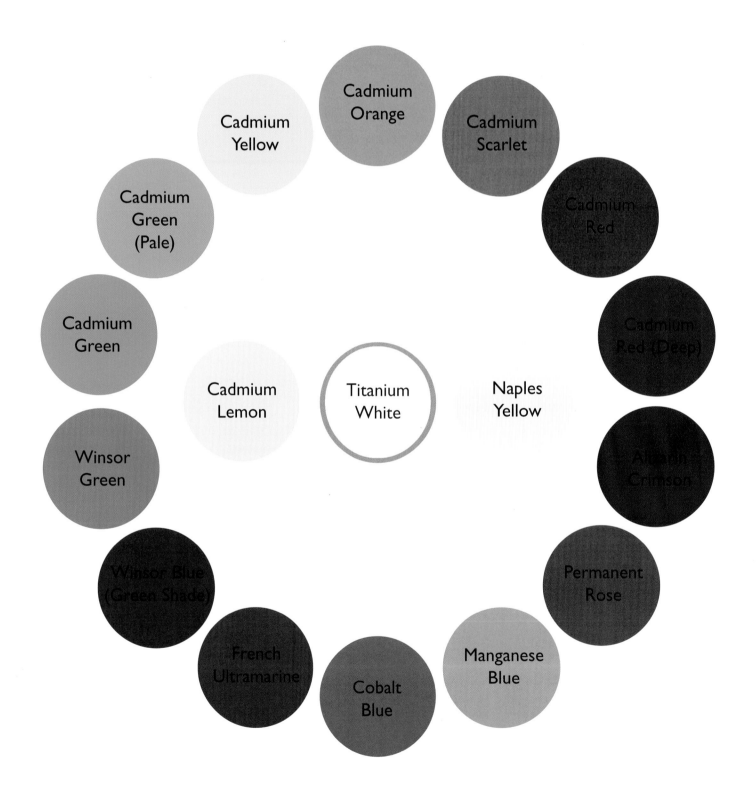

Cadmium Yellow

Cadmium Orange

Cadmium Scarlet

Cadmium Green (Pale)

Cadmium Scarlet

Cadmium Red

Cadmium Green

Cadmium Red (Deep)

Cadmium Lemon

Titanium White

Naples Yellow

Winsor Green

Alizarin Crimson

Winsor Blue (Green Shade)

Permanent Rose

French Ultramarine

Cobalt Blue

Manganese Blue

BORIS'S PALETTE

CHAPTER THREE

Backgrounds

The simplest way to explain what happens after the drawing and underpainting stages is for Boris and Julie to take turns in giving practical demonstrations. A point worth mentioning first, though, is that when thinning oil paints they use odourless paint thinner rather than linseed oil because it dries much faster and they generally have to work as fast as they can to meet deadlines. Also, they paint with a bank of alternating warm and cool fluorescent tubes shining over their shoulders onto the work. This gives a balanced light so they can get consistent results no matter what the weather conditions are at the time.

Their methods of working are very similar, which is not surprising as Boris taught Julie how to paint. But there are differences. They have slightly different ranges of colour on their palettes for a start and their different temperaments show in the ways they tackle painting. Julie, says Boris, is a lot more optimistic and fancy-free in her approach, and less meticulous with details like masking paintings; Boris is naturally more cautious, or at least inclined to consider the worst possible outcome when making choices. He is also more methodical on the whole, though when it comes to looking after brushes Julie is the careful one.

They use disposable palette pads for mixing paints so they can tear off the top sheet and start afresh with each new painting. This is mainly because they don't like to let the paint dry for more than three or four days because it then dries too quickly on the board and is difficult to work. Also, it means that each time they paint they have a full range of fresh colour to start with. It saves complication. The paint names given are the Winsor & Newton designations, because that is their brand of choice. OK, so now Boris is going first, starting, as he usually does, with the background of a new picture.

Boris: When doing a background you have to keep in mind what will happen in terms of the figures. If the main figure is backlit, there has to be a reason for this in your composition. Also, you want the figure to stand out against the background so usually you want quite light colours behind it – though not too light.

The Hedge Knight

The result of the stages described opposite

There are no fixed rules but here are the usual steps for creating a background: I start with a ½-in (1.25-cm) No 20 sable brush, seldom keeping the painting on the easel. I like to be in physical contact with it, so I rest it on my knee and against part of the easel or anything else that's handy.

I begin with a darkish brown by mixing Cadmium Scarlet and blue, using this as a neutral colour just to create a frame. As I move across and down the picture I use more and more scarlet and then Cadmium Orange because the idea is to create a sunset in the upper right third of the picture.

At this point I'm just applying paint, I'm not concerned with blending or anything, just getting colour onto the board. So after creating the brown frame I add in Cadmium Yellow, Orange and Scarlet to introduce some brightness. This part of the process is called blocking. There's not much of an attempt to render surfaces, I'm just laying down slabs of colour for blending later. Next I introduce some Winsor Blue and White for the patches of sky that will show between the clouds.

Working with the same combination of colours I then start filling in the background around the figures. It doesn't matter if the paint goes a little over their edges because that can be sorted out later. Then I move towards the castle at the bottom (see page 36).

The thing to keep in mind at this stage is that it is meant to be very rough, you're just trying to get a feel of the background, getting an idea of the colour values and so on.

Then I go back to where I started and begin to blend areas as the paint dries. At this stage there's no need to worry too much if something doesn't go quite right. You can always come back later on.

When I'm reasonably happy with how it's looking, I take a clean dry brush and start to clean up the sky. I'm not too concerned with the area around the branch because it's only going to be seen through the leaves and other details that will be added later. With a dry brush the colours get a lot smoother, and I try to keep the areas behind the figures as simple and plain as possible so they stand out.

Even after ten minutes the paint will have dried enough to behave very differently from when you first lay it on. Different colours dry at different rates, but this is something you just have to learn. It's important to keep a piece of cloth handy to clean your brushes as you go along because for blending you want to mix the paint on the board, not add any more. For that you use a different brush, such as in this case to add Lemon Yellow and White to the brightest areas of the background. The important thing is to keep your brush moving. Don't be afraid, just keep painting because if something doesn't work you can always come back and change it. If it looks like there is too much paint anywhere, just dip your brush in thinners and lift it off, then dry your brush and blend it as before.

At this point it starts to become clear why the figures have the highlighting that they do.

OK, so now my attention goes to the area on the left, which is going to be mostly vegetation. I block in some green and warm Cadmium Scarlet just to indicate colour, adding blue and more green as I come towards the lighter area. Vegetation is very random, I just lay down the colour and let it take shape on its own, keeping the darker

The Hedge Knight

Finished image, the finer details of the background having been added after completion of the main figures.

colours at the bottom. I used to use black paint for areas like this but something I learned from Julie is that it's much more interesting to use dark tones made from other colours. Then I add some colours to the rocks and the first stage is done. It doesn't take much time, maybe an hour or so. Then I clean my brushes and leave the picture to dry for a couple of hours.

Julie: I usually put most of these colours on my palette at the start of a painting even if they're not all going to be used, because you don't want to have to stop in the middle to add a new colour.

The thing to keep in mind about paints is that they are chemicals that sometimes interact in ways you might not expect. For example if you mix a cadmium colour with Titanium White the metals conflict with each other so it's not just a simple mixing of shades. Sometimes that's good, but you just have to experiment and get to know what to expect. Some artists are wary of cadmium because it's toxic, but we find it offers the

JULIE'S PALETTE

Tarot

Note how the sword fades towards the top to avoid distracting attention from the face.

richest shades of these colours and you can't beat them. Also the same colours from different manufacturers can work in different ways. You just have to get to know the paints you work with.

Almost always with a painting I start with the background because this establishes the colours that the main figures will have to fit in with. If I did the figure first I would then have to match the background with the figure, which is much harder than the other way round. Plus I'd have to worry about its edges.

With this painting the idea is that this is a troubled place, so it has a rocky landscape with a cloudy sky.

The rocks have diagonal lines that slow the eye down and give the picture more depth than horizontals would. Also, they form a contrast with the horizontal cloud layers. In the far distance there's a clear patch of sky to show that there is some hope here. That's where I'm going to start because with backgrounds I mostly like to work from farthest away coming forward. The attitude to take at this point is to go in and just believe what you are painting, so you can bring it to life.

In the distance there's always less contrast and difference of colour. In this case I'm starting with a light area and the hint of a sunset, but I don't want the colours to be too clean because I want to save those for the main figure. Also I know the rocks are going to be quite dark so as I'm working on the sky I take this into account. When it comes to mixing colours there are really no rules. You just have to experiment. You might mix two that make a dirty colour but often that's what you want. If you get it wrong you can always lift it off and try again. A general rule with backgrounds is to make them a bit greyish, because if all the colours in a painting are bright they have no significance. I also usually paint backgrounds thin enough so that any lines drawn on the board will show through. This lets light reflect through the paint off the board, but how thick to lay the paint on is something you have to learn by experiment.

You have to learn the different properties of all the colours you use. I didn't realize how different they all were when I started painting. For instance, the thing I like about Magnesium Blue is its transparency, whereas Winsor Blue is much more solid, so you can use it to glaze over areas. When mixing white with other colours it's best to start with a patch of white on your palette and touch in the others till you get the right shade, because you use less paint that way. I like to use Burnt Sienna as a base colour because the warmth shows through, whatever you paint over it. But although hints like these can be passed on, every artist has to learn most by trial and error, there's no other way. I can remember listening to other artists when I started painting and thinking: 'Gosh, how come everybody else knows what to do?' But everybody learns the same way – by experiment.

A general rule with brushes is that for really big areas you use large synthetic brushes, and for backgrounds a ½-in (1.25-cm) brush with natural bristles is right. Then you go to smaller brushes for details, but you have to just find what works best for you.

Returning to the picture – the next stage is the light sunset in the distance, but now rather than gradually darkening towards the stormy areas of the sky I then move to the darkest extreme and work backwards to bring them together. In this case, to lighten certain areas I'm using Naples Yellow instead of white to keep them warm. If I wasn't sure what to do with the clouds at this point, or if they start going wrong, I'd look up some reference but in this case it's going fine.

Now the colours have been put down I get a dry brush with long, soft bristles. Since clouds are soft they need to be blended that way, but I don't blend them evenly all over. I want it to look like an oil painting and not as if it's been done with a computer or airbrush.

After the clouds, I move on to the rocks on the right hand side, starting with an area where I know what to do. For these I use a stiff brush and if they're going to be brown I like to mix the colour rather than take it straight from a tube. All the time while doing the rocks I think about what's going to be in the foreground because that needs to stand out. Also, I separate the layers of rock by using different colours in each, laying them down quite roughly and making sure they are continued behind the figure where necessary. Introducing white makes the colour much duller where needed. Then when the paint has dried for a while I start pulling the paint off with a damp brush to define the rocks' contours.

A useful general rule is that the character of the brush you use determines the character of the rock; so round brushes produce round rocks.

Then I use a small brush to define the edges and shadows. Another useful general rule is that the more different sizes and types of brush you use on rocks, the more varied they will look. Also, as you approach the foreground the rocks will contain more contrasting colours. For misty areas of the background use a large soft blending brush

Because the light is coming down at an angle, the rocks on the other side of the picture will be much darker; but the colours of all the rocks have much in common with those in the clouds, just warmed up a little. Also the colours of the rocks on the left warm up as they come closer to the front. All the same colours will also be used in the skin tones of the main figure.

Often at this stage of a painting it's hard for an artist to keep faith that it is going to work, but you have to just keep going. A useful trick if you don't know what to do with an area is to cover it up with a finger or hand and your mind will tell you what should go there. After the background is blended in it's time to take a break, step back and view it as a real place. The aim is to get the background medium done, then do the figure, then go back and finish the background.

Wolf's Eyes
Finished image

Ice

1. Blocking out the background
2. Starting on the eyes and face
3. Completing the face
4. Completing the body
5. Finished image

CHAPTER FOUR
Main Figures

There are a few general rules for making foreground figures stand out by the use of brighter colours, sharper details and greater colour contrasts than in the background. Also the skin tones should reflect all the tones used in the background, otherwise the figure just looks as if it has been transplanted from elsewhere.

The most important element in the main figures of Boris and Julie's paintings is the face, which is where they usually start. Next we're going to look at two examples of how Boris and Julie bring faces to life, starting with drawings that have been transferred to board and underpainted with acrylics. Usually the background will have been already painted to half completion, but in Boris's example there is to be no background because the head and shoulders of his Wild Man are to stand alone as a T-shirt design.

WILD MAN FACE

Boris: With a face I always start with the eyes. There's no real reason, it's just the way I feel most comfortable. So with a small brush I mix up some Alizarin Crimson and Winsor Green to get a 'deepest dark' brown and then paint in the pupils and the lines around the eyes. At this point it's almost like drawing the features again. Then I start introducing colours to the face. The process is almost the same as with the background, I'm just laying down slabs of colour to be blended later.

Just next to the painting I tape a same-size print of the photo from which I'm working, and a pertinent point here is that we prefer not to work with colour reference. We shoot the model in colour but print out in duotone or quadrotone so it comes out in sepia. We used to work in black and white but found that, as far as digital cameras are concerned, quadrotone prints give a much greater range of tone values. The main reason for this is that we like to use our own colour schemes to suit the painting, and it's hard not to be influenced by what you see in a colour photo.

I block out the colours with a No 8 brush, starting with the darkest areas which are almost as dark as the eyes but with more scarlet. As I go along I may change the tone values if there seems the need. Also in this case I increased the intensity of the frown. I then introduce some bright colours, adding Cadmium Scarlet, before turning to the cool colours. He's to be a wild man so I give him some five o'clock shadow around the chin and upper lip by laying on some cool colours there. Also he's been running around so I give him pinker cheeks than normal. The lips are pinker anyway so I add that; and then, because the nose gets more sunlight than the rest and sticks out from the face, it needs to be a bit redder. As you put in colour on a face you don't just think of the colour but the tone values – where are your darker/ lighter areas? I put on some highlights with Naples Yellow mixed with white, and then do the whites of the eyes.

One thing to remember about the whites of eyes is that they are never as white as you imagine. Even in bright sunlight the only pure white in a face occurs when there are harsh highlights. Pure white does not otherwise exist; it is always mixed with other colours. I use a small brush for the whites of the eyes, using dark grey paint. At this stage I'm not worried about details, just blocking in colours to be blended later.

Here you see the end of the first stage, ready for the colours to be blended. It could almost be left like this but that's not the way I like to paint. From this point I start to blend the paint with a dry brush, being careful not to overblend because if you mix the paints too much they just form a muddy colour. I rub the blending brush off on a piece of cloth occasionally to keep it clean, and I leave some texture on the surface because it can look bland if you make it too smooth.

Wild Man Face
1. Blocking out the face

I

Up to this point everything has been free and quick moving, but now I'm going to start again at the beginning, moving in tighter. With a fine brush I sharpen up the eyes. In general terms Julie and I always start going from dark to light areas of a face. So now I pick out the eye lines – the brows and pupils – and at this stage I start polishing, blending more carefully. Normally I would use a new brush for this but this is a large face so it doesn't have to be that sharp.

2. Sharpening up the eyes

Most painters like to work on the whole figure and then gradually refine the different areas, but we prefer to do them section by section. I don't like to stop in the middle of a face but I can if necessary, and then come back to it.

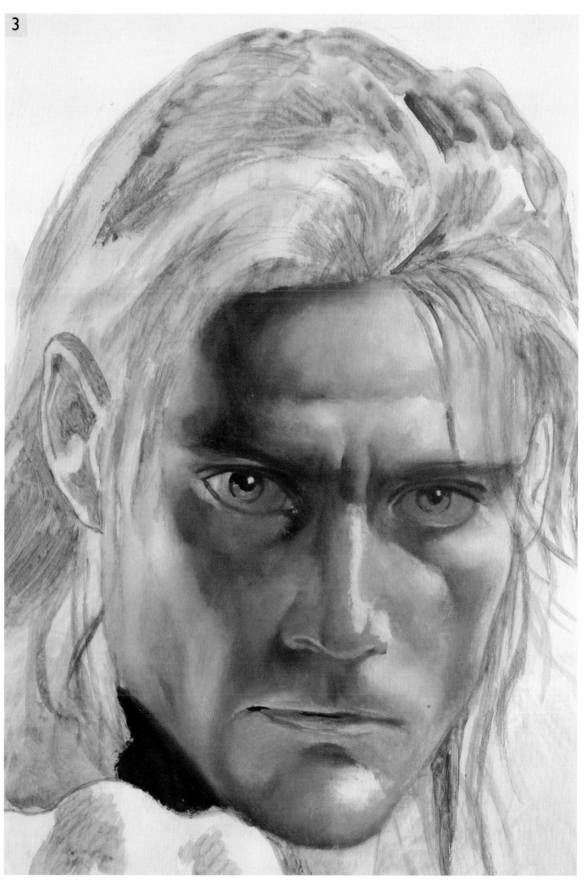

3. *Blending the skin*

Now I'm bringing out the highlights, keeping the colours cool on the backlit side and warmer on the rest, blending with a fine brush.

4

4. Adding highlights

And here is the face almost finished. At this point I often turn the picture upside down to view it purely as a colour composition as this often suggests final detail touches. Other tricks for seeing a painting objectively are to view it in a mirror, or simply to go away and leave it alone for a while. Usually when you come back the solutions to problems are obvious, and sometimes they have just disappeared.

5

5. Final touches

Wild Man Face

Finished image. The picture's title was chosen to avoid infringing copyright on any famous fictional wild men!

TAROT FACE

Boris and Julie have similar approaches to their work but there are differences. With a normal face Julie seems to build up the colours more gradually rather than laying down slabs of very different colours at the start. With both, though, painting is a very active drama taking place on the board. Once begun, their brushes are in constant motion till they reach the end of a stage. Here we see Julie bringing the face to life on the Tarot picture for which she did the background earlier (see page 38). She starts, as Boris did, with the eyes.

Tarot Face
1. Underpainted sketch

2. Starting with the eyes and blocking out the face

Julie: I usually start with the face and eyes of the main figure because they are the main focus of a painting. I also like to get some hair on there at the beginning because it helps to get the values right. I don't have to do all the hair – just enough to show how it's going to contrast with the skin. I start with the darkest colour I can get – mixing Alizarin Crimson, Winsor Green and Winsor Blue. I want to keep the shadows on the face warm though, so I hold back on the green for those areas and pick up some Cadmium Scarlet. Too much green gives a lifeless colour.

To begin with I work with the browns, just laying the colours next to each other without blending them. For the darker shadows I mix in Magnesium Blue, which is a transparent colour that is easy to control. For the lighter areas I add Cadmium Orange. I still haven't cleaned my brush, I just keep adding new colours to it. I always get in trouble if I don't put in something about the ears at this point. It's tempting to leave them till later but the colour is more consistent if they're done at the same time as the face.

Only when the main shadows are in place do I clean the brush and sit back to see how the picture looks. I'll probably come back later to darken some bits but the next thing I'm going to tackle are the reflections on the right cheek and nose, seeing how far I can take them.

3. Blending skin tones

I think that in the shadows it's nice to have what's called a 'lost edge' where the face blends with whatever's next to it and you can't see the definition. It happens a lot in reality so it's more natural that way. Also it's maybe worth mentioning here that the darker colours I've chosen for the face are stronger versions of the colours of the rocks in the background of the picture, while the paler areas use colours from the clouds. Those are the areas I'm tackling next, using the spots of colour on my palette that I mixed for the clouds, and adding Cadmium Orange to blend the lighter areas into the shadows.

When I was first learning to paint I asked Boris what colours to use for skin and he said 'just use any' because any colours can look right depending on the circumstances. It's better to go out on a limb and use really creative colours to start with, then tone them down if necessary till they look right. That's better than the opposite approach – being too cautious. You need different patches of colour on the painting to keep it from being monotonous. Also, over years of looking at people you learn that certain parts of faces such as the nose have more red than others, though you don't usually want to make your characters look as if they've been drinking! Any time an area starts to look too red, add some blue or green. And if it's too cool, add some red or orange. On female faces you have to beware of cool colours on the lower part of the face because it can look like a five o'clock shadow. With the whites of eyes you really have to study the values there and put down what you actually see rather than what you think you see. That's a general rule for painting faces, but it's particularly true for eyes. It's very easy for the mind to override your observation.

Although we use the background colours for painting the main figures, you have to be careful not to make the colours too similar as then the figure can start to look transparent – which can be really disturbing. As with everything in painting, you have to find the right balance by trial and error. In this case I mixed some Cadmium Green (Pale) and Cadmium Yellow into the highlights to make them stand out. For serious highlights I mix some white into the yellow but you have to be careful when using white because you hardly ever find pure white in nature. Even with something like clothing you're always looking at different tones of white.

Then I give some more attention to the eyes. It's more important than you realize to get them focused at just the right distance. When posing models we always give them something to focus on at the right distance or else they'll look wrong in the painting.

The lips I save for last because I really want them to stand out in this picture, I want to give something really punchy there.

When working on lips you shouldn't be afraid to use different reds (purplish, crimson) side by side because it looks more natural than just a single colour. Also I

Finished image. Final touches are still possible after the rest of the hair and headdress have been added.

soften the edges by blending because that's more natural than a sharp line.

While blending I keep wiping the brush off to keep it clean, and change it often. I tend to blend more in the lighter areas and less in the shadowed ones to provide contrast. At the blending stage you're still doing a lot of drawing because blending is not that precise and you have to constantly redraw the original lines that are now invisible under the paint. When most of the blending is done I usually leave the painting to dry for a while before coming back to work on the details. For realism it's really important to have a good photographic study of the face because the tiny details around the eyes, lips and nose make all the difference.

If ever you feel you're getting bogged down in an area, move on to somewhere else and come back to it later. Usually the problem will then be solved. The important thing is to keep moving. Problems can always be solved at the final stage of a painting when you come back and reinforce things that have got lost in the blending. The final stage with this face is to paint in the hair to check that it doesn't mess up the contrast. What shows is that the pupils of the eyes need darkening, so I do that and then the face is done.

ATTITUDE

What is immediately apparent from sitting in on these painting sessions with Boris and Julie is that despite their vast experience each new painting is still an adventure that they feel could go horribly wrong. The adrenaline in the air was tangible as Julie worked on the last face and at one point near the end she felt she had lost her grip of it completely (she hadn't of course, but had to take a break to realize this). Boris appears calmer but that is, he says, because he does his best not to think too much about what he's doing.. The fear is still there underneath.

Boris: One thing I have to have is classical music playing in the background, because I love music and my mind can concentrate on that. If I think too much about a painting I can be totally overcome with fear. So I'm not totally conscious of what I'm doing, I listen to music and let my mind go into outer space while my hands get on with the work. The mechanical part of me takes over.

Julie: A lot of people feel that once you're a professional the painting becomes easy but I still feel some fear every single time I sit down to a new picture. But perhaps it's a good thing because it might get boring otherwise. Maybe fear is one of the necessary components of art.

Boris: But I do just love sketching because then there's no pressure. You can go endlessly

Birds of Prey
1. Initial face sketch

1

2

2. Blocking out the face and hair colours

3

3. Starting to blend colours

over and over a sketch, changing things till they look right. With a painting, although you can change things right up to the end, it's much harder work and you have more to lose if it goes wrong.

Julie: There's also a certain amount of luck involved in getting a painting right because of how the colours are laid down. The skill is knowing how to use lucky accidents, but there's also always the fear that luck might go the other way.

Boris: One skill is learning to be your own worst critic. You always have to be trying to do better than before.

Julie: But we feel that anyway. Even if you love a painting, at the end you can always see how it could have been better.

Boris: Although we always feel we can do better, experience is a great help for judging if a painting is going in the right direction. The problem is if you can't see what's going wrong. That is probably the most important thing for an artist – the ability to see what is wrong with a painting. We mentioned some tricks earlier for distancing yourself from a picture – turning it upside down or viewing it in a mirror – another trick is closing one eye. It sounds funny but flattening the real world like that somehow makes the flat surface of a painting appear more three-dimensional. It also helps to have a partner who is also an artist. In fact we have a whole family of artists because our sons are painters too, and we all offer and ask for criticism. They're able to give us informed criticism but in fact anybody's opinion is valid.

Julie: Since our work is commercial we need a wide audience to like it.

Boris: But the first person you have to please is yourself. Then if you're lucky you find an audience that shares your enjoyment.

4

4. Fine blending of skin tones

Birds of Prey

Left: 5. Finished face

Angel Rides

ODDS AND ENDS
STONE DRAGON

Sometimes, even after a painting is 'finished', Boris and Julie will need to go back and make minor or even major changes. This can be at the request of an art director or it can simply be that the painting just doesn't feel quite right. This painting underwent several revisions. Before any of these pictures were shot, the girl with the torch was a completely different model. The art directors were happy with the general pose and body of the girl, but they wanted her face to be more consistent with the character in the book. Julie repainted the head using photos from a different model. The next problem was that the dragon on the wall in the background was supposed to have been carved out of obsidian. The first attempt to revise this rather major change in the background was done with the computer. Julie then realized that the only way to get the effect she wanted was to go back and simply repaint the background. At the end of the day, the new "finished" painting is certainly more dramatic and captures the look of the heroine precisely.

Stone Dragon
Detail above
Opposite: 1. Painting with modified heroine

I

2. Improvement prior to attempted computer manipulation

3. Final image with repainted obsidian dragon

THE COMPETITION

Julie: The texture of fur is not really any different from skin. What I did with the wolf here was block out the dark and light areas and then blend with a soft brush just as for skin. Then I went in and just indicated some of the hairs. You don't want to put in every individual one because too much detail would distract the eye from the rest of the painting. I used the same range of colours for the wolf and the lady so they would appear to be in the same scene. It's important to keep your light consistent, especially when, as here, the reference pictures you're working from were taken in completely different conditions (meaning that I didn't start with a picture of this girl and the wolf running through some woods!).

After the main figures were painted I softened and lightened the background to make them stand out. I also chose bright red for her hair to catch the eye because it's the opposite of all those greens. I'm not sure I'd want to hang out with this lady because she looks kinda scary. I gave her a mask like the wolf's to show their affinity.

To get the feeling of motion I used a tip I got from some books about comic art – they tell you to choose the most exaggerated point of an action because otherwise it can look flat, even if it is exactly how the action looks in reality. You have to focus on the idea of the movement more than any action shots you may have taken with a camera.

The Competition
Detail above

I

I. Underpainted drawing

2

2. Background blocked in and half-finished

3. Wolf's fur being blocked in and rendered

3

4. Note how the edge line along the wolf's neck creates a sense of texture

Opposite: Finished image. Basically the same range of colours was used for both wolf and female

THREE OF SWORDS

Here's an example of how to create a sense of temperature through the use of paint. The first picture looks warm and could easily be set in some baking desert. The next stage immediately establishes the setting through the introduction of blue and white. Also, more subtly, the coldness is conveyed by the sharpness of clouds and other details in the distance. In a warm setting they would be blurred by mist or haze.

Three of Swords

1. Underpainted drawing
2. A feeling of temperature is introduced through colour and sharpness

3

3. Main character portraits set the tone of a picture as much as the rest put together.
Opposite: Finished image. This painting is from an ongoing series of unusual tarot cards.

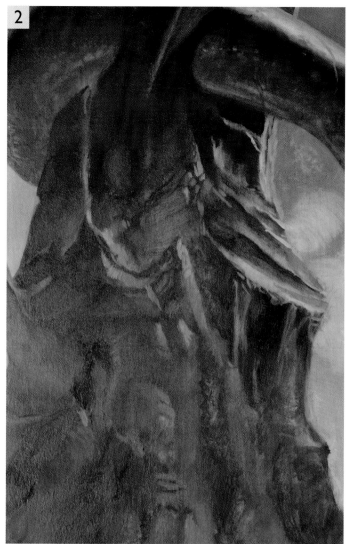

He-Man

1. Main figure
2. Detail of mountain
3. Detail of creature. Note
that in fantasy the teeth
of monsters and villains
are usually exaggerated.

CHAPTER FIVE

Case Studies

In their calendars Boris and Julie have pretty much a free hand in what they paint. Usually they agree a general theme and range of pictures with their publishers first, but beyond that there are no restrictions and no need to get client approval as a picture progresses.

Most of their paintings, however, are commissioned pieces with very specific ends in mind and they need to be approved by clients at every stage. So what follows are some examples of how they go about this. The first is a self-contained book cover. Then come three linked pictures for an advertising campaign. Before we start, here are a couple of general tips from the artists regarding commissions:

Boris: With a new client it is important to be sure you are always both clear from the start whether they are buying the actual picture or just the right to use the image.

Julie: Often Art Directors say they don't know what they want but when you ask a few questions it turns out they do have something quite specific in mind. Also sometimes they just assume you know what they want without explaining themselves. So before you start work the thing to do is ask questions – and then more questions until you find out what are the exact limits of the assignment!

HE-MAN

Julie: This tiny little drawing is shown almost life sized. We start really small to get the feel of the composition, using those little yellow stickyback notes about 3 in (7.5 cm) square. Our first drawings are little doodly things to get an idea of the composition.

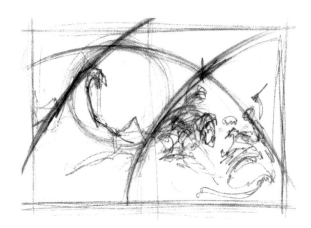

Boris: This was a little different from usual. Our pictures are normally vertical but this was to be a double page spread for a wraparound book cover. At this point we already had a list of characters and elements requested by the client. What we were looking for was a sense of how it was going to work in terms of the concept.

Julie: In the first sketch you see the red and blue lines holding it all together. Also you can faintly see the circle that will become the moon in the final picture. When doing a composition you'll see repeated shapes and movements. Here the main character repeats the red curve over on the left.

Boris: Once we've established the general idea we begin to define each element. The next stage is refining the gestures, deciding what to do with each character. In this case the two characters are confronting each other so we tied them together with an S shape. One leads directly into the other.

1. *Second stage rough sketch*

Julie: It's important to create lines that keep the eye in the picture.

Boris: Yes it's really important for defining a composition to make the eye go where you want.

Julie: Also at this stage it's important to keep the drawing loose and swirling. You don't want to make tight little drawings. You're describing the action not the elements. Compositions are like dance, graceful, dramatic or whatever. The details come later.

2

2. Rough figure studies on separate pieces of tracing paper so their interaction can be adjusted

Boris: Here we're starting to define the elements within the composition, more often than not on tracing paper, so we can move them around. But these days we also sometimes do this on the computer in Photoshop.

Julie: The figures are drawn separately so they can be moved around in relation to each other.

Boris: Here the figures are much more resolved as a sketch. This is not just to show the client for approval but for us to see where the picture is going. Although we start with a concept, every painting takes a direction of its own and you have to let this happen while staying within the limits of the brief.

3

3. Figure sketches close to completion

Julie: This was quite a complicated painting. There are several things going on and they have to work together as well as each half being able to stand alone on the two sides of the book.

Boris: Here the sketch is taken to a fairly finished state to see how it will look. The dark sky was dropped in with Photoshop to show a certain amount of depth. You can see Snake Mountain still facing away because that's how our reference showed it, and we just placed it there as it was.

4. Sky dropped in on the computer to get a feel of depth in the final picture.

Julie: You can see why the snake needs to face inwards because like this it just draws your eye away from the main figures. We're so conditioned by art over the centuries to read pictures from left to right, even if we aren't aware of it. Maybe it comes from how we read writing, but even in other countries where the writing goes the other way pictures seem to work from left to right. When seeing covers of books the ones that catch the eye usually play on this.

Boris: In the next picture (see page 84) you can see the moon positioned so the snake head will be silhouetted against it when it is turned the other way.

5

5. Moon dropped into the background for sketch submitted to clients for approval.

Boris: In the finished painting the main figure was further emphasized by blending his opponent with the dark foreground, making a frame around him. Also you may notice that the proportions of the picture have changed, making it slightly taller to fit the required format.

Julie: You have to keep the composition flexible right to the end to allow for this sort of change.

He-Man

Above: Finished image. Snake Mountain has been reversed to draw the eye towards the
battling figures.
Left: Detail of background

OASIS

This was an interesting project for Boris and Julie on a number of fronts. It began with an email from a London agency, Mother London, which wanted to use their work for an ad campaign for the Oasis fruit drink. The idea was to introduce fantasy elements into everyday settings using some of the artists' existing pictures, but it was soon decided to go for original art. Boris and Julie also decided to tackle the project together, which is surprisingly rare, and came up with the three scenarios that follow, using familiar shots of London provided by the agency as backgrounds.

One challenge was that the results were to be used in a variety of formats – billboards, magazines etc. – with different proportions. So it was decided to create the three main elements of each one separately and then bring them together at the end in a balanced way for each format, along with the required lettering.

So the main figures were painted on white backgrounds to make them easy to lift and put in place, using Photoshop on the computer. Boris and Julie have never had any formal training with this program, which intimidates many people, but say the truth is that even if you are only using 1% of its capability that doesn't matter as long as it gets your job done. There's no need to take a course to understand the other 99% of its possibilities, unless you need to for your work.

CLOUD ACCOUNTANT

The first dilemma here was getting the character of the accountant right and you can see from the sketches (page 87) how he evolved. The first, well-muscled one seemed too serious so they decided to make him older and funnier. But that went too far in the opposite direction so they settled on a character that was somewhere in between.

The next decision was over whether to simply use photography for the background, but it was decided a painting would look better because the softness of a painting would blend better with the fantasy element.

The computer came in handy to incorporate the figure in with the clouds. It was necessary to blend the figure with the soft clouds in a seamless way, using transparent layers and shadows.

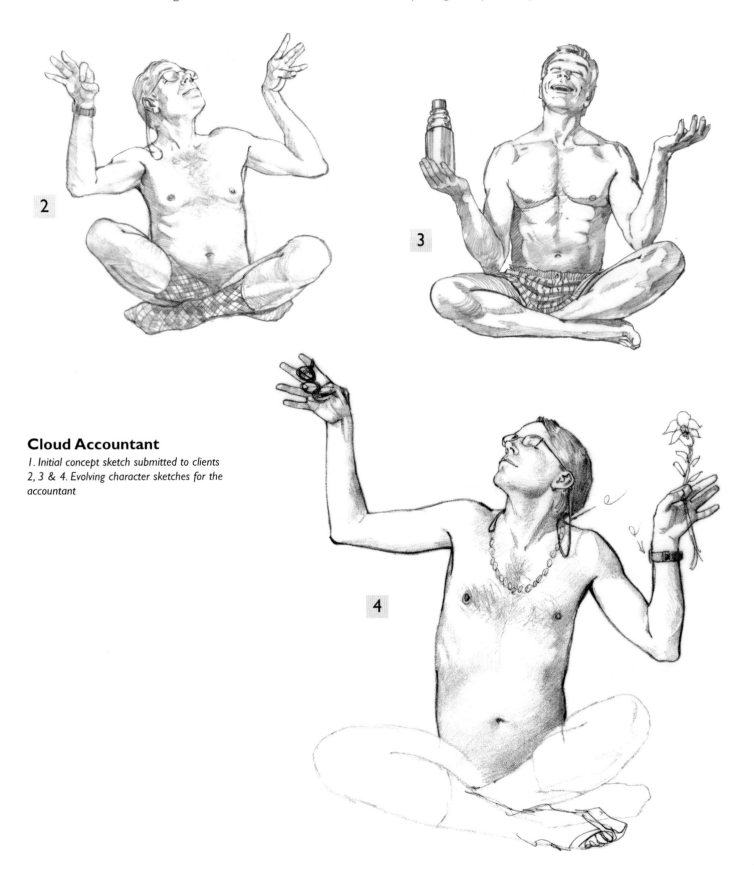

Cloud Accountant
1. Initial concept sketch submitted to clients
2, 3 & 4. Evolving character sketches for the accountant

5. Acrylic underpainting of background

6. Done

7. Detail of clouds

8. Detail of clouds

9. Semi-finished background painting

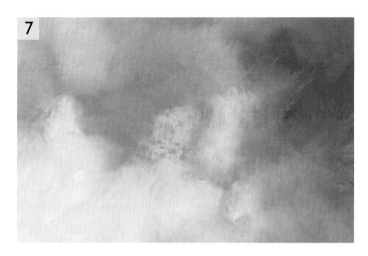

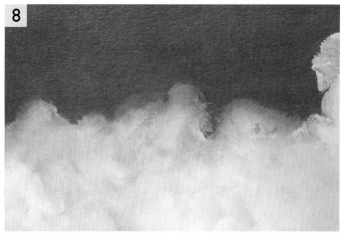

10. Detail of London cityscape

11. Detail of London cityscape

Illustrations on pages 90–91 produced for the Oasis brand. Reproduced with permission of the Coca Cola Company in the UK.

12. Finished background painting

13. The model for the meditating accountant was a computer wizard friend of someone Boris and Julie know from the gym. He took it as a great compliment being asked to star in one of their pictures, as opposed to their more usual muscular subjects.

Cloud Accountant

Finished image: Apart from lettering and a bottle of the Oasis drink this is the painting as it appeared on billboards around the UK.

Illustration produced for the Oasis brand. Reproduced with permission of the Coca Cola Company in the UK.

FAIRY OF THE PARK

Boris: In this kind of situation the computer has the advantage of allowing you to position elements wherever you like against a background, but you also don't want them to look as though they have just been pasted on. For instance, this fairy has to reflect the surroundings in her skin tone. In isolation her face looks like it has quite strong green tones but these disappear when she is put in place. Now, granted you can make adjustments to tone in Photoshop but it looks much better if they are painted in from the start. The perspective also has to be taken into account. So on the one hand the computer can simplify a job but it also creates another set of complications.

Julie: You have to visualize the figure in place even while working on it separately. Also in a painting the edges of a figure are not completely sharp, so once it is placed in Photoshop you blend in the edges with the Blur tool. There are other refinements too such as adding shadows and reflections into the background.

Fairy of the Park

1. Freehand character sketch

2. Concept sketch submitted to clients

Boris: An important difference between painting and art done purely on the computer is that computer art lacks the personality that comes from creating something completely with your own hands. For me it's important to show your personality in your art – it has to look as if it comes from your own hands. For instance, our textures are made up and random in a way that cannot be done on a computer. So for us the computer is a tool that can help finish off a composition, but the art is created by hand.

3

3. Background sketch in acrylics with elements mirrored so that the tower does not clutter up the area in front of the fairy

4

Illustrations on page 96–97 produced for the Oasis brand. Reproduced with permission of the Coca Cola Company in the UK.

5

4. Introducing colour

5. Introducing trees as a dark background to set off the main figure

6

6. Detail of background

7. A technical problem was getting the perspective right so that the man and his dog would not look like midgets when the fairy was dropped in overlapping them.

7

8

Illustrations on pages 100–101 produced for the Oasis brand. Reproduced with permission of the Coca Cola Company in the UK.

9

8 & 9. *Details of fairy's face*
10. *Some grass was added below the fairy to help blend her with the background.*

10

Fairy of the Park

Finished Image. With added lettering this is how the picture appeared in some formats – the man and his dog being happily blind to the touch of magic behind them.

Illustrations on pages 102–103 produced for the Oasis brand. Reproduced with permission of the Coca Cola Company in the UK.

FAIRY OF THE UNICORN

Here we see London's famous (or infamous) Millennium Dome in the background. It was decided not to give the fairy wings because the unicorn immediately tells the viewer that they have strayed into fantasy territory.

Fairy of the Unicorn

1. A problem with the Dome was that the artists have never visited London and had only a fuzzy snap to work from, but luckily, being in the background, it meant that detail was not too important

2. Freehand sketch for the concept picture submitted to clients

3. Freehand sketch of unicorn

4

4. Blocking out face colours

5

5. Blending paint on the face

6

6. Finished portrait

Illustrations on pages 106–107 produced for the Oasis brand. Reproduced with permission of the Coca Cola Company in the UK.

7. However hard-headed the commission, Boris and Julie usually find space within its parameters for personal artistic expression.

8. Their talent is knowing the boundaries within which they are allowed to please just themselves. In fact this is probably why their brushes are so much in demand.

9

9. *Main figure dropped into sketchy background to test colour values*

Fairy of the Unicorn

Finished image: Lacking only lettering and Oasis bottles

An interesting point to note here is that, as with the backgrounds of these pictures, it was decided that the bottles of drink shown in the adverts should also be painted, even though they were to look as realistic as possible. Keeping their use on billboards in mind, they were painted larger then life-sized with as much fine detail as possible. Julie painted one and Boris the other, starting from the same drawing. The small lettering was handled in Photoshop because the edges needed to be perfectly crisp and clean.

This sounds easy in theory but in fact created a whole set of new problems in getting the curvature and perspective right. These extra lengths demonstrate the perfectionism they bring to their work. This applied also to the care they took in painting each bottle separately, instead of just doing one and then changing the colour with a click of the button in Photoshop. The reason for this was that the transparency and texture of different juices is also quite different, so they wanted to show that.

Stages of painting the two bottles showing the different textures and transparency of the juices

FANTASY CREATURES

Dark Whispers

'Even completely fantastic creatures like dragons have to be based on something real.'

Julie: The thing to realize about fantasy creatures is that although they come largely out of your imagination they have to be based on something people recognize.

Boris: They have to have believable muscular structures, for which we draw on the experience of what we've painted before – both from human beings and from existing animals and insects. Even completely fantastic creatures like dragons still have to be based on something real because things don't come out of nowhere. I often give my dragons basically human musculatures while Julie's are usually based on animals. The choice depends on what message you want to convey to the viewer.

Monster Bash

Mood is established by colouring as well as body language.

Julie: For instance in the dragon you see bowing to the lady opposite (page 110) Boris used the exact pose of a submissive dog to give a subliminal clue to what's going on in the picture, while the creature's fierce eyes, size and spikiness indicate that in other circumstances it could behave very differently. The rest of its body is a composite of various real creatures.

Power Armadillo

1, 3 & 4. 'Our starting point was three sketches for the client to choose from, humanizing the character to make it really threatening.'

Boris: If you contrast the dragon (page 110) with the smaller creatures in the picture beside it (page 111) you can see that the dragon is a creature that moves slowly whereas, from their body language, the others look like they move like lightning. You get this not just from the images themselves but from how they interact with the human figures. All elements are intimately connected.

Those two pictures also show the importance of colour in setting the mood of a picture. They basically use the same colours but applied in a different way, the dark colours of the first picture being softened by the use of pastel shades to create a touch of gentleness. In the second they're kept hard.

Julie: If Boris had wanted to make the dragon even more submissive he would have given it softer eyes. Or for a really cute dragon he could have given it human eyes and less spikiness.

Boris: The concept behind the creature opposite (page 112) was that an armadillo is the mascot of the company that commissioned the painting – a manufacturer of stereo casings. There's nothing threatening about real armadillos of course, but the client wanted us to exaggerate the idea of the armour's toughness by making the creature really tough and mean too. So besides giving it a shell of steel we added some spines and gave the armadillo some attitude.

Our starting point was three sketches for them to choose from, humanizing the character so we could make it really threatening. Textures are really important if you want to get realism into a fantasy picture. You really have to study and analyse them.

Julie: People often write in asking how do you do this texture or that. We don't mind giving tips but really there is no other way than spending hours and hours analysing them. It helps to see how other artists have managed it but really you want to look at good examples of the textures themselves and work out your own way of doing them. Then you can simplify and exaggerate as much as you want.

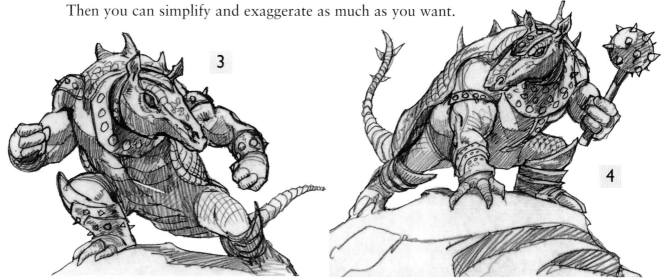

Scorpion

1. Background detail
2. Foreground detail
3 & 4. Details of creature

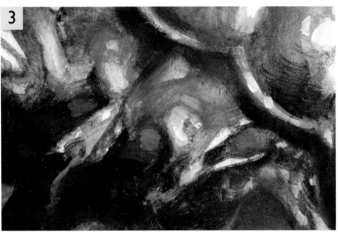

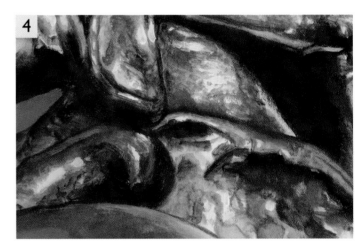

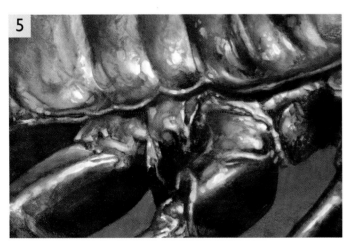

5. The main reference for this scorpion was actually a little bronze sculpture, but the problem this raised was that Boris had to work on changing the reflections because the metallic ones were far too harsh.

6. Luckily he has a couple of scorpions (dead) in his collection and got a wonderful satisfaction out of bringing the three together in this painting. It shows.

Scorpion

CHAPTER SIX
Painting Metal

As Julie just said in the previous chapter, it's often impossible to explain in detail how she and Boris achieve their effects, but there are tips and pointers that can show the way to anyone with the talent and perseverance to follow them up. One of her own particular skills is portraying shiny metal surfaces and it attracts so much comment that here we have a step-by-step demonstration of how she does it. It's not recommended that any beginner starts with anything as complicated as a face though. A shiny doorknob or old-fashioned chrome hubcap would be a much more manageable bet, but the principles are just the same. To get a feel for the subject she recommends taking a lot of photos of such objects out in the open on a clear day to study the patterns of reflections. It's easier to do this from a photo than just by looking at the objects themselves because photography flattens the image, removing the distraction of three-dimensionality.

Two points need to be made clear before Julie starts, though. The first is that she does not use metallic paint. A surprising number of people, including other artists who should really know better, think that she does but no, she just uses the colours on her normal palette that we showed earlier. The other point is that the idea is to create the illusion in the viewer's mind of seeing shiny metal, not to recreate exactly how it would look in the scenario of the picture. This is why painted metal often looks harder and shinier than a photograph of the real thing. It is a kind of trick being played on the eye and mind.

No special measures need to be taken at the sketching stage for an object that is going to be turned into shiny metal. In the example she's chosen here Julie only decided to make the lady metallic at the last moment before painting, because it suited the Tarot card character she wanted to portray. So the first face shot shown here (page 116) is her drawing on board shaded with acrylics in preparation for being given perfectly ordinary skin. To this she then just starts applying a different range of paints to those she had intended. The thing she has to say next explains the whole trick in a nutshell, though there is of course a bit more to achieving her results in practice.

Queen of Cups

1. Underpainted figure ready for oils

Julie: If you're just learning to paint shiny metal it's best to assume that your object is lit from above, because your brain is used to seeing shiny objects that way – outside in the open with the sky reflected in the top half and the ground in the bottom. Plus when you see opposite colours reflected on the same surface your brain knows that it is shiny.

2

2. Sharpening the eyes

Julie: I start by applying some Winsor Blue mixed with a little Cadmium Red, because I want it to be blue but not too bright. Then I add some white and define some of the outlines. With metallic objects you always get a bit of bright additional reflection along the edges, which you can see here along the nose, cheek and forehead. Also I'm leaving a line along the top of her forehead that will reflect the colour of her hat. The thing you have to be aware of when painting metal is that it's not going to come out as you want right away. This is hard for a lot of artists to start with but it doesn't matter, it will take shape. Often I almost have to try not to look at a painting too hard at this point because I might freak out.

3. *Getting bold with the blue*

Julie: So now I'm going to go straight into the highlights. I'm probably going to touch in other highlights at the end but this will establish where the picture is going. I start with the blues and lighter colours first to keep them clean. This is the opposite of painting a normal surface when we usually start with the darker and warmer areas and move into the highlights. The trick is to keep your brush moving and not get too scared because you're not going to start seeing what you want till the colours are all in there. What I'm doing is blocking in the cool areas reflecting the sky, using blue even if the painting's sky is going to be something else – because blue is what your brain expects to see there on a shiny surface. I'm not aiming to reflect the surroundings exactly, just enough to create the illusion.

4

4. Initial blending of the bright areas

Julie: Now I'm going to start going into the warmer colours, mixing Cadmium Red (Deep) and Winsor Green. I skip around the face rather than trying to finish one little part at a time because that keeps it all consistent. I'm not sure what to do with the eyes yet but when the rest is done something should suggest itself. At this point you have to just leap in and go for it, if anything goes wrong you can always come back and fix it later. Then I paint in the edge of the hat where it's going to reflect on the face, and the reflection in a lighter shade. The difference will be greater when I finish the hat later because it will be both darker and more textured than the reflection.

5. Getting bold with the brown

Julie: Sometimes the colour gets a bit smudged here and there at this stage but often it's good to leave these 'happy accidents' in because they add a bit of authenticity. I'm blending the blue areas as smoothly as possible into the really light highlights to get the effect of a really clear sky being reflected. Some of the highest highlights get lost during this, but I'll come back and reinforce these later if necessary when the paint has dried a bit, so it doesn't matter. The smoothness is more important.

A curious thing is that if you copy all the lines and details of a photographed reflection into a painting directly, the result comes out looking wrinkled and uneven, so you have to simplify for a good effect. If I'm not sure where the reflection is going to go, I apply the paint really thin so it can be lifted off if necessary. At this point I've decided to make the eyes realistic.

Now I'm going to take Cadmium Orange and go into the darker reflected areas. It's a bit scary but this goes back to what we said earlier – that if you have two very different colours reflected on the same surface you realize that it's shiny. In this warmer area I'm not blending as smoothly as in the other half because this gives another kind of contrast to look at; also because the warmer area is supposed to reflect the ground, which is not as smooth as the sky. I'm also introducing some yellow but there's no strict formula for the colours to use here, I could just as easily go darker. An interesting thing to try in areas like the right cheek here is just to add several different colours at random into your brush and see what comes. It adds a bit of variety as if some interesting feature is being reflected there.

Julie: 'At this point I've decided to make the eyes realistic.'

Opposite: 6. The dark areas can be much more rough and varied than the light ones.

6

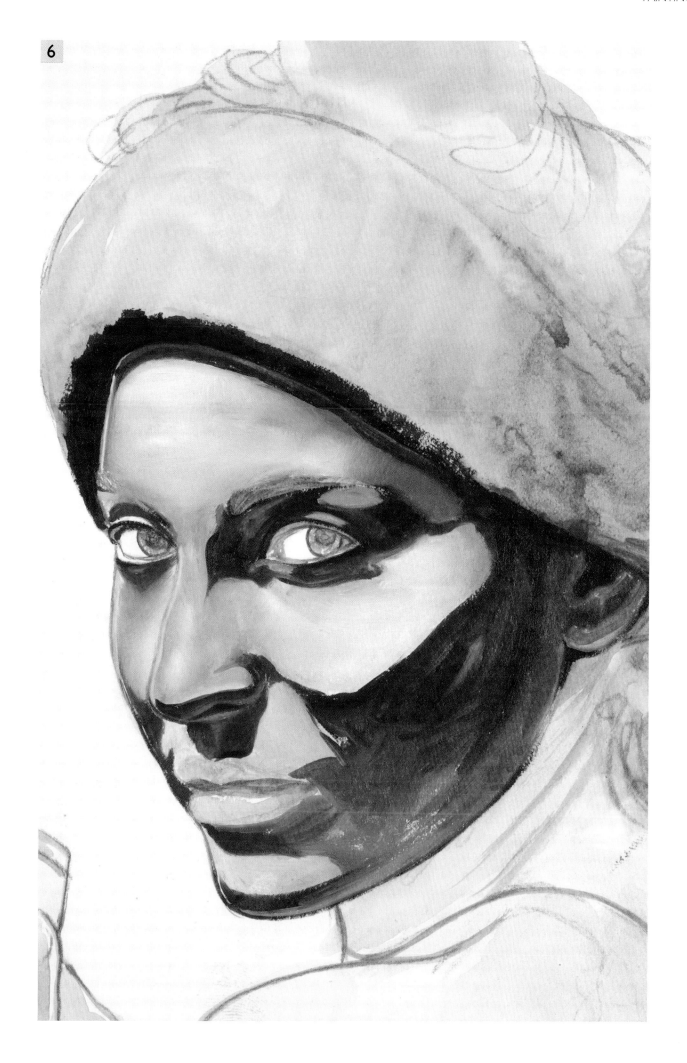

Now I'm blending the darker areas, balancing between keeping it interesting and not letting it get too weird so the face starts to look lined. Then I move onto the lips, which I've decided will be bright red. Normally I blend the edges of lips into the face because they look more natural that way, but here there's going to be a sharp line. Her teeth are showing slightly, which presents a problem. Teeth are always tricky unless you're dealing with a bad guy or a monster, when you can exaggerate them as much as you want. Otherwise it's best to minimize both the teeth and gaps. And here we have the metal face more or less finished apart from details like the eyes, which I'll come back to later.

7

7. Chromed face almost finished. Final touches can be added later

Queen of Cups

Finished image. Note the eyes.

1

Pink Metal

1. At this point either the horse or the heroine could be turned to metal

Opposite: Finished image. Hey presto! Just follow the steps given earlier and you too
can do this!

Julie: A question we often get asked at conventions is whether we have any secret short cuts to doing the kind of work we do. The short answer is that there aren't any beyond what we've been able to show in this book. There's no way round having to just work at your art until you are happy enough with it.

Another point we make with students is that if they want to be professional artists they are going to be competing with others, so they have to get out and see what other artists are doing. Often artists are a bit sensitive and shy about doing this, and in school they're too shy to ask questions, but being a professional is very different to just doing your own work at home. You're not just competing with yourself, even if you're doing Fine Art – that's the reality.

Boris: A point I feel is really important for young artists is that talent is a necessity but it's also only the beginning of getting somewhere with art. Hard work and tenacity are what then make the difference between someone who is good and one who is outstanding. Talent can even be a handicap for those that rely too heavily on it and neglect hard work and persistence.

Another thing is the importance of experiment. You have to see what will happen for yourself and not be afraid to make mistakes, because they're often the best way to learn.

Julie: Also we tell students that nothing can replace the basics you learn at art school. Besides the techniques there's also the criticism you get from teachers and other artists. It's very important to learn to take criticism and put it to good use, not take it personally and get offended. You can use criticism to strengthen your art – it's a gift.

Boris: Yes, learn to be analytical about your work, and other people's too. You have to ask yourself 'Why do I like this? Why does it work?' Because, sure you can get feedback, but ultimately the choice must come from you. Then after being analytical you must put the analysis behind you and paint from your heart.